THE REAL SALVATION

Bert M. Farias

A Holy Fire Ministry Publication.
Printed in the United States of America.

ISBN: 978-0615610382
Library of Congress data is available for this
title.

TABLE OF CONTENTS

The Great Deception   1

The Philosophy of Satan   21

A Holy Invitation   45

THE GREAT
DECEPTION

Consider these statistics of Christianity in America. Eighty-four percent of the inhabitants of this nation say they believe in the deity of Jesus Christ. Seventy-seven percent believe their chances of going to heaven are excellent. Thirty-three percent believe one day everyone will go to heaven. Over 90 million Americans, nearly one third of our nation, claim to be born again Christians.

Yet America has the highest percentage of single-parent families in the industrialized world, the highest abortion rate, the highest rate of

1

sexually transmitted diseases, the highest rate of teenage birth by far, and the highest rate of teenage drug use.

Consider also the great moral decline of the last generation (40-50 years) and these telling statistics in America. The divorce rate has doubled, teen suicide has tripled, reported violent crime has quadrupled, the prison population has quintupled, the percentage of babies born out of wedlock has risen six-fold, and couples living together out of wedlock have increased sevenfold. And many believe that the end is not in sight.

These statistics are eye opening and they serve to warn us that something is terribly wrong with our brand of Christianity. They reveal how poorly the Church has communicated the true gospel to mainstream America, and thus the reason for so much deception in our culture.

When the rich man died and went to Hades (Lk. 16:19-31) he was surprised to find himself there. In the Jewish culture they equated wealth with godliness, so this man thought God favored him. The common thought, especially among the Jews, was if you were blessed financially then you were a good person, and therefore you were going to heaven. This also explains the disciples' astonishment when Jesus told them how hard it was for the rich to enter the kingdom of heaven (Mat 19:25).

Similarly, there was a church in Laodicea (Rev 3:14-22), who due to their wealth, thought they too had attained God's favor. Jesus expressed great disapproval over their spiritual condition as well, which they were totally unaware of.

Are you in touch with your true spiritual condition? Or are you allowing the pop culture around you to dictate your standards? Are you conforming to the world's standards or to the Bible?

How can a nation of people among whom a large percentage claims to be "born-again" Christians experience the kind of degradation the above statistics reveal?

The answer is rather simple: The real gospel has not been preached nor lived. Both the *profession and the practice* of the majority of so-called Christians in this nation have not matched up. Our substandard message has produced substandard believers. Our departure from the preaching of the cross, repentance, holiness, and the real empowering grace of God has increased the level of deception in the church. We desperately need a restoration of the real spirit of Christianity.

One Christian media consultant revealed the reason for the watered down version of the gospel on America's airwaves. "There is very little substance and weightiness to it because people have an appetite to only hear about goodness and prosperity, but are repelled by any message of personal responsibility that requires something of them."

Ministries cater to their viewers so they produce what their itching ears want to hear. After all, they reason, "this is a business and we've got to give the people what they want, especially since they are the ones paying for the broadcast." Whatever happened to ministering in the "sight of God"? For a number of years now we have been reaping the consequences of a faulty gospel, and that's the reason for a faulty harvest.

The definition of the real salvation has been blurred. And for this reason also our culture is filled with deception, and apostasy is increasing at an unprecedented rate. It's much worse than what many have even thought. The Church is in dire need of revival. And the nation is in desperate need of a spiritual awakening. True Christianity is transformational.

Let's start with the basic doctrine of salvation. There are varying opinions. We have libraries full of sermons and yet still so much confusion and deception about what a real Christian is. Have you ever had anyone lie to you and deceive you? I've had people lie and deceive me and take my money. It made me angry, but losing your money is not the end of the world. Money can always be replaced. Deception that takes your money is costly, but deception that condemns your soul is fatal.

Some have said, "Hell will be filled with good people." What a shock to get to the end of your life, having been deceived by the culture around you, and like the rich man in Luke 16 and the church in Laodicea discover that you've been practicing religion instead of righteousness! What a shock it will be to many professing Christians when their spirits leave their bodies at death and they are denied entrance into the kingdom of heaven, and instead find themselves in a place called hell for all of eternity. Can you imagine feeling secure in a salvation you don't even possess? Only real Christians will enter the kingdom of heaven. What then is a real Christian?

Let's begin by first identifying what a real Christian is *not*. Here are the three most common beliefs in our society: 1) One who simply agrees with Christ's or the church's teachings; 2) One who attends a particular church or denomination; 3) One who is morally good. None of these definitions are accurate, but yet this is what most of the culture believes.

Now how did Jesus define what a real Christian is? *"UNLESS A MAN IS BORN AGAIN HE CANNOT SEE THE KINGDOM OF GOD"* (John 3:3). This powerful statement from the lips of Jesus removed any and every other way of seeing the kingdom of God. Born again people are the only kind of Christians there are! However, to many people in America and around the world "born again" is just another denomination. So the question needs to be:

WHAT DOES IT REALLY MEAN TO BE BORN AGAIN?

"*I will give you a new heart and put a new spirit within you; I will take the heart of stone out of your flesh and give you a heart of flesh. I will put My Spirit within you and cause you to walk in My statutes, and you will keep My judgments and do them.*"

(Ez. 36:26-27)

Let me be very plain:
A born again Christian is a person who has a new heart and a new spirit from God. Once he receives Jesus Christ he receives new desires. He begins to hate what God hates and to love what God

loves. The habitual desire to sin is removed from him. His sinful nature is taken away and he receives the life and nature of God in his spirit. This is the greatest miracle! Without it every man is separated from God for all of eternity, and does not possess an inner grace and power to be Christ-like in this life.

The reason a real Christian cannot keep living the same old way is because he has the nature of God, the very seed of God, abiding in him (1 John 3:9). He cannot tolerate sin in his life. Birds do not swim, fish do not fly, and a real Christian cannot habitually practice sin. To do so would be to go against his new nature. A lifestyle of sin is totally incompatible with the seed of God. For a professing Christian to love sin and continually make every effort to enjoy sin is proof that he is not born of God. Proof of the new birth is a new life.

Once that incorruptible seed (1 Pet 1:23) is sown within a man, a tree will come forth from his life that bears good fruit (Mat 7:16-20). You know a real Christian by his fruit (his behavior and actions.) There are many who profess Christ, but in works they deny Him (Titus 1:16). A real Christian seeks to please God in thought, word, motive, and deed. It is his nature!

What a person *does* comes out of who he is. The basic problem with every human being is that they are rotten in the core of their being. They have a sinful nature and a general hardness of heart. It does not matter how morally good and clean they seem to be on the outside. There is a huge difference between a morally good person and one who has God's nature and has truly been born from above.

In the sight of God the best of mortal man's deeds are like filthy rags and polluted garments (Isa. 64:6). It's not by works we are saved, but by God's grace through faith, and that not of yourselves; it is the gift of God (Eph. 2:8). Say that last phrase over and over again; not of yourselves...not of yourselves...not of yourselves. God only accepts what He Himself has done to regenerate a man. God sent His Son, and he that has the Son has life (that is the nature of God), and he who does not have the Son does not have life (1 John 5:12). It's that simple.

There are only two kinds of people in this world: Those who have the eternal life of God in them and those who do not. There are those whose hearts have truly been changed by God's power and those who have not. It is really all a question of a person's spiritual condition. There can be no mixture. You're either born again or you're not.

There is no such thing as a Methodist Christian, a Baptist Christian, a Catholic Christian or a Pentecostal Christian. God is not a Catholic or a Protestant or an Evangelical. He is not a Hindu, a Buddhist, or a Muslim. He is not a Mormon or a Jehovah's Witness. Those are man-made labels to identify people and their religious persuasions. God did not come to this earth in the form of man to start a new religion. He came to give us life! Away with religion and give me life!

Here's another truth: God did not create you and I for sin and evil. He created us to have His life. He created us to be holy and righteous. In the beginning He imparted to man His life and nature, and then restored that life and nature to man through the cross. You cannot have God's life and nature until you believe on the Son of God, Jesus Christ.

One of the problems in Christianity today is that the word, 'believe', merely means to acknowledge God's existence, but in the Bible believe implies obedience. God gives eternal salvation and His Holy Spirit to those who obey Him (Heb 5:9) (Acts 5:32). Not only does God inwardly transform us by giving us a new heart and a new spirit (nature) through his amazing grace, but He also gives us grace to obey. Notice the second part Ezekiel 36:26-27 again:

"I will put My Spirit within you and cause you to walk in My statutes, and you will keep My judgments and do them."

The new nature from God will work obedience in you and cause your walk to match your talk. You will keep God's Word. You will do God's Word.

Once a person dies and his spirit leaves his body it is too late to alter a person's nature and birth change in him. To say it another way, at the time of physical death a person's spiritual nature is irreversible. His spiritual condition will remain the same forever. It is only in this earthly life that it can be altered.

"He who is unjust, let him be unjust still; he who is filthy, let him be filthy still; he who is righteous, let him be righteous still; he who is holy, let him be holy still" (Rev. 22:11).

"Do you not know that the unrighteous will not inherit the kingdom of God? Do not be deceived. Neither fornicators, nor idolaters, nor adulterers, nor homosexuals, nor sodomites, nor thieves, nor covetous, nor drunkards, nor revilers, nor extortioners will inherit the kingdom

of God. And such were some of you. But you were washed, but you were sanctified, but you were justified in the name of the Lord Jesus and by the Spirit of our God" (I Cor. 6:9-11).

No one with a sinful nature can inherit the kingdom of God. Sin and holiness can never touch each other. When someone flippantly says, "I'm going to hell because that is where my friends are," he is telling the truth. A man with a sinful nature could never survive the pure and holy atmosphere of heaven. So if a professing Christian down here on the earth enjoys hanging out in a place where evil and lustful passions rule, and where sin abounds, then his nature has likely never been changed, and he is still in his sins.

Being born again is a radical transformation. It is a miracle of great proportions. To professing Christians everywhere, let us not cheapen the grace of God with definitions and a lifestyle that are not worthy of real Christianity. And let us not frustrate the grace of God by not yielding to the new life and nature of God by which we've been changed. Once again, true biblical grace gives us both the *desire* and *ability* to live in obedience to God.

If enough professing Christians in America heed this message, we could have a national awakening unlike anything we've seen in the history of our nation.

THE PHILOSOPHY
OF SATAN

Atheism says there is no God. Islam says there is a God, but he has no Son. Catholicism says there is a Son, but His mother must be worshiped.

But Jesus Christ said, *"He that has seen Me has seen the Father...and he who honors the Son honors the Father"* *(John 14:9)*.

Satan's philosophy is to take honor away from Jesus Christ, and to make sure He is not glorified. He seeks to put Jesus on the same level as all other gods. He seeks to offer the world a variety of substitutes for the true salvation, and to be tolerant of all religions.

But Jesus said, *"I am the way, the truth, and the life. No one can come to the Father except by Me"* (John 14:6).

Have you ever wondered why the world refers to God in general terms, but when someone mentions the name of Jesus everyone gets nervous? Have you ever wondered why men use Jesus Christ as a curse word and blaspheme His name? And yet no other founder's name or god of any other religion is used that way!

Why is that? It is because, *"There is no other name under heaven whereby a man can be saved except by the name of Jesus" (Acts 4:12).*

As we said earlier, Satan tells people that God is a Catholic, or a Protestant; or that He is a Muslim, a Hindu, or a Buddhist. His greatest strategy is deception. He works persistently to distort the true image of God and the gospel. Satan is a liar and the father of lies (John 8:44).

God is a God of truth. His foundation is truth. The Church is called the pillar and ground of truth (1Tim 3:15). The main responsibility of the Church is to bring people into agreement with the true and living God.

23

One of the central truths of almost all religions is that sin separates man from God. However, that is where the commonality of all religions ends because every religion differs in the means by which man is reconciled to God.

In most religions man must do something to reach God---everything is based on a system of works. In Christianity it is God doing something for man. *"While we were yet sinners God sent His only Son to die for us" (Rom 5:8).* No other religion can boast of this depth of love and redemption.

THE BLOOD

The most important truth about Christianity is the Blood of Jesus Christ. The Blood is what reconciles man to God. Satan and all demons hate the Blood!

There is no approach to God without the Blood. There is no favor with God without the Blood. There is no fellowship with God without the Blood.

The Blood is the heart of God.
The Blood is the central theme of the Bible. The Blood is the thread and fabric of all history, civilization, and time.

The blood of every animal offered on sacred altars in Old Testament times was to reveal Jesus Christ, the Lamb of God, slain from the foundation of the world. The Old Testament sacrifices teach us that God requires blood to cover sin; a life for a life.

In society we have a law and justice system. For every crime there is a penalty. God also has a law and justice system. The penalty for sin is death. In order to cancel death a life had to be given.

In creation God breathed into man's body the breath of life (Gen 2:7). And that life was carried in the chemical substance called blood. The life of the flesh is in the blood (Lev. 17:11).

Before Adam sinned he carried the life of God in his blood. Scientists cannot explain the mystery of blood and its capacity to carry life. That is why at death a human body gradually grows cold because the life has departed from the bloodstream.

Through Adam's sin, corruption, death, and decay was introduced to the human race and the bloodstream of man became contaminated.

That is why in Old Testament times there was to be a daily shedding of animal blood to atone for the sins of the people. A daily shedding---leftovers would not do. This was to emphasize how much value God places on blood.

During special times such as the Passover there was to be a lamb sacrificed for every household so that death and destruction would pass over them. Over 2 million people needed to sacrifice approximately 150,000-200,000 lambs to receive deliverance. That's a lot of blood!

During the dedication of Solomon's temple it is recorded that the sacrificing of sheep and oxen for the atonement of people's sins were so many that it, "could not be told or numbered for multitude." That's even more blood!

In 1500 years of Israel's history before Christ, it is impossible to compute the amount of shed blood. The brook Kidron where excess blood was dumped was fed with so much blood that it flowed with the color red for days.

Why so much blood? Because God was trying to show Israel that the value of blood cannot be measured in quantities of gallons or dollars and cents. No amount of animal blood could offer the kind of atonement we needed for our sins. Animal blood only covered man's sin, but did not have the power to transform him. No amount of animal blood could take away our sin nature and free us from spiritual death. Something else had to come.

Enter Jesus!

What is it that makes the Blood of Jesus so precious and powerful?

Consider His birth. The virgin Mary, whom God had chosen to give birth to Jesus, did not supply the ovum, but it is written that God prepared a body for Jesus (Heb 10:5). This is talking about Jesus being conceived within Mary and taking on human flesh.

Jesus pre-existed eternally with God the Father, but He didn't stay in heaven or in the Spirit. He left heaven and took on the form of a man of His own creation that he might die for our salvation. Not even the angels understand this kind of love, that Jesus would strip himself of all heaven's glory, honor, and authority to become an earthly man in order to redeem man.

When God prepared a body for Jesus the human factor in a pregnancy was erased. There was no Adamic blood from Mary. The blood was not mixed. God imparted His own life into the bloodstream of Jesus through the agency of the Holy Spirit.

That is the reason the Blood of Jesus is holy and precious. In essence, it was God's Blood.

It is highly important to understand that the category of Jesus' Blood was very different from any other human blood. It is priceless. It was God's price for the redemption of the whole human race. This is also why the consequences for rejecting it are so severe.

Someone once compared salvation to a blood transfusion. Imagine if transfusions from Jesus' Blood could be kept in blood banks. Everyone who would obtain a transfusion of Jesus' Blood would actually be receiving

God's eternal life in pure and holy blood.

This is not how salvation is administered, however. But a miracle just as great takes place when a man puts his trust in Jesus Christ for his salvation. Immediately, a powerful cleansing happens, and the sin that is in the bloodstream of man is purged.

The danger of intellectual theology lies in allowing the shed Blood of Jesus Christ to become a historical fact rather than a present day powerful reality. We must turn our passive theological faith in the Blood of Jesus into a vital and active faith.

There is more power in the Blood than anyone has ever imagined.

Now do you understand why Jesus is in a unique category all by himself? Now do you understand why Satan fights the person of Jesus Christ with such vigorous efforts? Now do you understand why Satan uses religion, tradition, and laws to conceal the truth and power that is in the Blood of Jesus Christ? It is said that somewhere in the world Satan invents a new religion every year.

Now do you understand why laws are made to remove prayer, the Bible, and crosses from our educational systems and public forums? Now do you understand why throughout centuries of time Jews and Christians have been the most persecuted people on planet earth? Because from them came the law of God, and the prophets, and finally the person of Jesus Christ.

Satan opposes Jesus Christ!

Jesus Christ did not come to found a religion. He did not come to establish an earthly institution or organization. He came to accomplish one singular mission. He was sent by God to bring man, who was made in His image, back to God. That's why the devil hates Him! And that's why he hates us!

"God was in Christ, reconciling the world unto Himself" (2 Cor 5:19).

Jesus Christ is the only One who ever completely satisfied the great heart of God by satisfying the claims of justice. He is the only one who paid a full price for our redemption, not with corruptible things such as silver and gold, but with His precious Blood. Jesus fulfilled every wish and every requirement of the heavenly Father. Adam, Noah, Abraham, Moses, Elijah, David and every other man of God has failed to do this, as well as any founder of false religion.

Jesus Christ submitted Himself completely to God, surrendering every part of His being and will into the hands of the heavenly Father. Jesus never spoke a word, never committed an act, and never performed a miracle for selfish reasons. All He did was for the glory of God.

When He was hungry He could have turned stones into bread but He didn't because it would've dishonored the heavenly Father. But when He taught a multitude of 5,000 men and knew they were hungry, He took 5 loaves and 2 small fishes and multiplied them and fed them. He performed this miracle, as all others, to glorify the Father.

Jesus walked and talked for the honor of the Father. Jesus taught, worked, and healed for the honor of the Father. Every contribution He ever made in

37

His earthly life was for the honor of the Father.

No man ever lived like Jesus lived. He was sinless. He was faultless. He was spotless and without blemish.

"Yet He who knew no sin was made sin for us" (2 Cor. 5:21).

Amazing! Incredible! And almost too grand and glorious to believe---that the Creator of the universe gave His precious life for His sinful and fallen creation! He offered a solution to the sin problem once and for all.

Sin is in the bloodstream of every human being. It is the reason for every rape, theft, lie, murder, and suicide. Sin is the reason for every illicit sexual act and every form of crime. It is the reason we have wars and strife, broken homes, drug addicts, alcoholics, battered wives, and abused children. Sin is the reason for prisons and hospitals, policemen and funeral parlors, and false religions and cults.

And it is the reason that Jesus Christ, declared to be the Son of God, came to this earth!

No man ever loved like Jesus loved.
No man ever served like Jesus served.
No man ever suffered and died like Jesus suffered and died.

He was the greatest human being who ever lived upon the face of this earth.

However, His birth, His life, His ministry, and His miracles could never have helped us and saved us without His precious Blood being shed on the cross. Had Jesus failed in even one point, His death and His Blood would've meant nothing.

There have been many religions since Adam. There are hundreds of religions and cults today, but the Bible declares that there is one Lord and one Faith... one Way, one Door, one Light, one Shepherd, one Mediator, one Truth, one Life!

Try and imagine the absolutely most glorious and explosive human being that ever lived.

Even though He was born in humble circumstances, to a peasant girl, in a barn where animals are fed; in His body the express image of God and the brightness of His glory was contained.

Imagine Him waking to the rising of the morning sun that He Himself created. Picture Him walking on the earth His own hands formed. Follow Him as He is baptized in the waters He set in motion. He is the Creator!

Now picture Him as He had His final conversation with the heavenly Father (recorded in Heb 10:5-7) before being born of a virgin girl on the earth. See Him walking through the corridor of heaven with angels on either side of Him bowing down before Him. As the Son of God leaves heaven the gravity of what was about to transpire was suddenly realized by every single angel.

The Creator was leaving His heavenly home to become one of God's creations! Stepping out of the intense light of God's throne and walking away from the glory of the Father, Jesus Christ heads toward the earth as all of heaven stands at attention. Awe and wonder fill the hearts of the multitude of angels as they realize that the creation of the universe, which they had all witnessed in the beginning of time, now pales in comparison to the Creator leaving heaven to become one of His creations. All this He did to redeem us so we would not perish but instead have everlasting life.

How can any human being resist this kind of love?

Then sings my soul, My Savior God, to Thee...how great thou art! How great thou art!

A HOLY INVITATION: "COME UNTO ME"

"Come unto Me all ye that labor and are heavy laden, and I will give you rest. Take My yoke upon you, and learn of Me: for I am meek and lowly in heart: and ye shall find rest unto your souls. For My yoke is easy and My burden is light" (Matt. 11:28-30).

The words above spoken by Jesus are some of the most beautiful in the Bible. They have been ringing in the inner courts of my heart lately and they call to every man, woman, and child. Everyone needs the Lord. Everyone

45

wants to belong and be counted as valuable and precious. Love calls and invites all to come to Jesus. He alone can answer and help and heal.

The road of life can be hard and heavy, but with Jesus, the yoke becomes easy and the burden light. To be true partners with Him means to bid farewell to the hard and heavy burdens of life. Truly, Jesus has come to lift our hearts. Can't you feel Him now and sense His tender loving-kindnesses? They are yours, my friend, because He is yours!

Oh this wonderful Jesus has given us of Himself! When you come to Him and call on Him from a sincere heart, you shall have His undivided attention. The Son of God bids us to come and walk with Him, and He will give us rest. How glorious and altogether lovely He is to me! Oh that all men would know of the depths of His boundless love!

Jesus strums the cords of my heart and reveals His excellence unto me as I in turn reach for Him just to say "thank you." But somehow those words still fall short of how grateful and appreciative I am for just "Him", yes, only Him and Him alone. Don't you see my friend that if we have Him, we have it all? We bow before Him and lift our hands to Him, but it's still not enough! Deep calls unto deep and the passions of my heart yearn to find a fuller measure of expression and praise.

Jesus is everything. Life is only worth the living because He lives. You lose your job, your relationships, and your possessions, but you still have Him. He is sufficient for your total satisfaction. You need nothing more. He is closer than a brother. Jesus is more than enough. Life is big, rich, and wonderful because of Him. "Come unto Me" is, and always has been, and ever will be His only call to unfulfilled humanity. If obeyed, you will find it sufficient.

How wonderful Jesus is to the heart whose sole quest in life is grounded in loving Him! How dear and indescribably precious He is to those who have truly made Him Lord and Master! Oh how my spirit rejoices in His love and tender mercies! Even as His holy Blood has washed me from all sin, so I now too minister to Him and worship Him with my love and adoration.

The eyes of my understanding have seen the Lord of creation, and so now His inspiration prances within me like a young colt loosed from the limits of his reins. Jesus has given me life, life, and more life! I was dead in trespasses and sins, but He breathed into me the breath of His very life! My heart was like stone, but Jesus rolled away the stone and gave me a heart of flesh! It is the miracle of new birth dawned within me by His own Word. Oh how utterly real He is to me! How can I tell you? How can I show you? How can I prove to you the nearness of His holy presence? This is not religion, but just Jesus; the One and only True Salvation offered by our God.

Jesus is a friend who sticks closer than a brother. Friendship does not mix with formulas. There is no set pattern for time with a friend. It is all spontaneous and free; full of surprises and glee. This Friend has only plans of heaven for me.

How could I ever mistake the rules and regulations of religion for the love and friendship of the Lord Jesus? What an insult to mistake the spirit of religion to the absolute, unassuming, and accepting nature of Jesus! How ridiculous to confuse that which binds to that which looses! How totally futile and worthless have been man's attempts to reach God! No man has yet reached Him. It is God Himself who has reached and revealed Himself unto us.

Only fools and those void of wisdom look for God in mountains and statues, and balls and beads. Only spiritual "goofies" could ever believe that God is only in Mecca, or in Jerusalem, or somewhere in India, or in some temple made with human hands. Only the disillusioned could actually conceive the idea of God being a Muslim, a Hindu, or a Catholic. How degrading man's carnal concept of God is! God is everywhere and yet in only one place will He reveal Himself to you, and that is in Christ Jesus. It is only when you've received Him that you find the favor of God, and your very own body becomes the temple of the living God.

Jesus Christ is so near to all who put their trust in Him. The crying or calling out of your faith to Him can set you free from all sin. The cross of Jesus Christ is where all of humanity is divided. The cross is also where man is reconciled to the presence of God.

The presence of Jesus is so complete and fulfilling. Nothing else can fully satisfy the broken aching heart of man. Religion has never done it. It is just Jesus that we need. He walks with me, this I know, and I long to share Him wherever I go!

Oh friend, listen to your heart and tell me what you hear. It is the love of Jesus speaking in your ear. He speaks to you and says: "Let Me come into your life. Let Me love you like nobody ever has. Let me fill you with My peace and holy joy. Don't be afraid for I AM GOD and I have come to save you and not condemn you. My precious Blood I've shed for you. What more could I do?"

Can you hear the longing of the heart of Jesus to bless you, friend?

Jesus Christ is easy. He is light-hearted, not legalistic. He is favorable, not overbearing. He seeks and searches out the souls of men. He dines with sinners and reveals Himself to them. When they see Him as He is then they repent of their sin and wickedness and bow down before Him. Take a good hard look at Jesus and He will melt your heart. Remove your traditional glasses and see Him for who He really is.

He loves you, friend. You are the apple of His eye. He came for you. He died for you. He shed His precious Blood for you. He is a personal Savior.

You are of great worth to Him. Don't perish. Let Him save you. Don't hide. Come to Him as you are. He sees you and knows you and longs to be the King of your heart.

Surrender to Jesus now, and the bitterness in your belly shall be turned to sweetness.

All would be lost without Jesus. All of life would be lived in vain. An empty bubble would be our world, and true joy a hopeless quest. The answer to everything is simply just Jesus. There is no other way to God except through Him. He alone can save, help, and heal. There is nothing you need outside of Him. All provision is found in Him.

Only believe and you shall see. The eyes of your understanding shall open, and you will know what millions have known the world over. Jesus is life!

Remove all obstacles that would prevent you from coming to Him. Knock them over! Push them down! Root them out! Shove your way through peer pressure and pride! Shut off the voices of reason, doubt, and skepticism! Turn your ear away from public opinion, and the skeptical voice of popular friends and relatives!

Every soul must find Jesus for himself. This is a matter between you and God. Jesus is the prize that every wise runner seeks. Sell it all and buy Him. Then you will have it all.

STEPS TO REAL TRANSFORMATION

1. Be real with yourself and with God. Stop living in sin and deception. Surrender to Jesus through repentance and faith.

2. Quit living independently of God.

3. Get a Bible and start reading St. John's gospel in the New Testament and go on from there. Ask the mighty Holy Spirit to help you understand what you read.

4. Find a real church with real Christians who actually live the Bible.

5. Write to us and let us know of your decision.

Holy Fire Ministries
P.O. Box 4527
Windham, NH 03087

www.holy-fire.org

Made in the USA
Charleston, SC
15 June 2012